Bygone BELLSHILL

by

Rhona Wilson

Bellshill Main Street looking East about 1908.

Main Street, Mossend

First Published in the United Kingdom, 1995
By Richard Stenlake, Ochiltree Sawmill, The Lade, Ochiltree, Ayrshire KA18 2NX
Telephone: 01290 700266

ISBN 1-872074-59-6

INTRODUCTION

The original village of Bellshill went by a different name entirely. Formerly known as "Crossgates", the village stretched from the present Bellshill Cross to Thorn Road and consisted of just six cottages. These dwellings housed workers from the nearby Orbiston Estate and were situated to be close to the estate entrance, along the present Motherwell Road. How Bellshill got its name isn't completely clear. There was a draw road from Bell's Quarry nearby (now Philip Murray Road) and it is thought to derive from that. There was no mention of it as a place name in historical records, however, until 1836 and a map of 1804 clearly labels the area as Crossgates (this name is still in use today for a stretch of road south of the Cross). Suffice to say, "Crossgates" became "Bellshill" on local maps by 1810, possibly for no other reason than a sleight of a map maker's hand.

In the late 1700s the surrounding parish of Bothwell, of which Bellshill is positioned roughly in the centre, was still principally rural. Hand loom weaving, with a grand total of 113 weavers, was the main occupation in the general area and the First Statistical Account listed a mere 50 colliers. Over the course of the century the relative importance of these industries changed considerably. Many weavers lost their jobs with the introduction of new machinery and steam processes in the 1840s. Coal, which was initially required to feed the furnaces of the adjacent iron-works, became a local industry in its own right. The exploitation of deep-lying seams of coal in Bellshill began in the 1870s and, with 20 pits in operation, coal-mining was easily the main source of employment.

Iron and steel production were also central to Bellshill's industrial development. J B Neilson, creator of the revolutionary hot blast process, opened the first iron works in the area (Mossend Iron Works) in 1839. This plant became one of the largest producers of malleable iron in Scotland and other iron works followed with Clydesdale opening in 1870 and Milnwood in 1872. Steel production using the open hearth process began at Mossend in 1880. Although the following years brought further expansion, a strike beginning in late 1899 and lasting a mammoth 14 or 15 months ended in the closure of the works. They were eventually re-opened by William Beardmore and Co. in 1906, with production peaking during the First World War when the works employed 3000 workers. Clydesdale works initially produced iron strip for tube making but also began steel manufacture by the open hearth process in 1884, supplying steel for the second Tay Bridge in 1885. The works continued to prosper with a series of company mergers leaving the plant owned by Stewarts & Lloyds in 1903. In 1925 a Universal mill was installed. This was the largest and most modern in Europe and increased production at the works by 50%.

The population of Bothwell as a whole grew in tandem with industry, increasing by over 100% from 19,292 in 1871 to 45,904 in 1901. During this period Bellshill became distinctly cosmopolitan. The numbers of Lithuanians immigrating to the town were so high that local traders, such as Austin the Baker, began to produce dual-language adverts. Many came specifically to the supposed promised lands of towns like Bellshill to work as labourers in the collieries, iron and steel works but it is thought that some merely stopped en route to America and settled here instead on account of the living to be had. Lithuanians in Bellshill even tell tales of some getting off the boat at Dundee believing they were in America. Although generally accepted by the indigenous community, two official complaints about their presence were made by industry representatives. In 1887, the Trade Councils of Edinburgh and Glasgow protested that Lithuanian workers were being brought into the district by the coal and iron masters, Merry and Cunninghame. Further complaint was made in 1901 at the annual conference of the Scottish Miners Federation that safety standards were being compromised by the inability of some Poles and Lithuanians to speak English. The immigrant community thrived regardless establishing its own bakery and general store (Varpas Ltd. at 104-116 Main Street) in the early 1900s and publishing a newspaper Iseivin Draugas (Friends of the Immigrants) from 1901. In the 1920s, between the two world wars, Lithuania was independent from the USSR and a second drove of Lithuanians were tempted over to Scotland again because of the job shortage in their own country. This was in the days of the General Strike in Britain and some were unwittingly used as strike breakers by the Coal Lords. The end of the Second World War saw Lithuania again under Soviet control and this was an incentive for many immigrants to stay in their adopted homeland. Even today there is still fear about returning to Lithuania among older members of the community.

The industrial boom which attracted these exotic incomers didn't last. A social and economic survey compiled in 1947 showed that 70% of Bellshill's male population was unemployed in 1934. In September 1930 a local commenting in The Bellshill Speaker warned that the town was "in danger of being evacuated by its inhabitants". The closure of the Orbiston Colliery in 1925 heralded the decline of the coal-mining industry. The industry in Lanarkshire as a whole had been in decline since before the First World War and what coal seams there were were either worked out or the coal uneconomic to retrieve. The mines closed steadily throughout the 1930s and 1940s with Thankerton at Holytown the last in the general area to go in 1953. Formerly, in 1924, the mines combined had provided jobs for around 8400 workers. The steel works also began to close as the demand for steel fell. In 1932 Stewarts & Lloyds moved the Universal mill from the Clydesdale works to a plant they were building in Corby, taking 670 jobs with it. Ironically, the Second World War revived Bellshill's fortunes for the duration. Steel manufacture was stepped up at Clydesdale for shell production and, even after the war, the plant survived making tubes for oil pipe lines.

In recent years light industries have taken over. In fact, for a time in the early 80s, Bellshill was famous chiefly for exporting light entertainment. Native pop singer Sheena Easton, hit The Big Time courtesy of an ITV programme of the same name. 1986 saw Kibun, a Japanese sea food factory, open in Bellshill Food Park. The company manufactures for the domestic and European market and currently employs around 130 workers. A local business park was also opened in 1993 to attract business to the area. The Cultural Centre (incorporating a library, cafe and rooms for exhibitions or community use) opened in 1989 and is a new focal point for the town. Bellshill's housing expansion has been engineered throughout the years by the building of a number of housing schemes. Orbiston housing estate, a self-contained community with its own shops, schools, churches and playgrounds, was built during the 1950s. More houses were added to it in the 1960s and building work commenced on private houses in the area in 1981.

Old Bellshill and the days of the rural estate of Orbiston it grew on may seem far away but there are reminders of that time, even today. In 1825 a daring socialist experiment was carried out in the area by A J Hamilton and Abraham Combe based on the ideas of Robert Owen of New Lanark. The Orbiston Community, a housing scheme with its own businesses, school rooms, theatre and so on was built with the intention of being run as a cooperative. Known as

"New Babylon" by locals on account of unorthodox Sunday habits, the venture floundered and dissolved after 3 years. The streets of the present Orbiston housing scheme, however, are named after the community and act as a permanent reminder. Thus we have Community Road, Babylon Place and Register Avenue (the latter being named after the community's newspaper). Although short-lived and long gone this distinctive piece of Bellshill history remains an integral part of the town today.

Old Men's Rest, still in use today, lives up to its name in this picture of the Cross in the 1950s. Kilpatrick's Public House once stood on this site but was demolished when the North Road was widened in 1937. Toll gates would have been positioned across the Hamilton Road here and only removed after tolls were abolished in 1844. Windsor Place, on the corner at the right, was built by Archibald Scott who went on to set-up a thriving coach building business. He saved the lintel from the thatched blacksmith's shop which originally stood there. The placard bearing the date 1777 can still be seen today, on the back entry door.

Stewart & Lloyds built the Clydesdale Works Institute in 1908 to provide an indoor recreation space for their employees at their Clydesdale Works. Carfin Hall (bought in 1923) redressed the balance by catering for more athletic pursuits such as tennis and football. This philanthropic gesture became redundant in 1932 (along with many of the workers) when the company moved the key Universal mill from the Mossend works to a plant they were building in Corby in Northamptonshire. Use of the facilities declined and the Institute was sold to the Lanarkshire Education Committee as a Junior Instruction Centre in 1935.

GOLF CLUB HOUSE AND 18th. GREEN, BELLSHILL

A 8424

Bellshill Golf Club was formed on 2nd May 1905 with 60 members. Expansion of the Greens to 18 holes took place in 1919 with the Club House being added in 1924. In an early handbook the club described itself as "an oasis in a desert of industrialism". Less picturesque, but fascinating nevertheless, was the discovery made by sewer contractors in 1930. They uncovered two beehive shaped chambers under the South Field which were later proved to be part of the sewage system of the Orbiston Community project abandoned in 1827. With 660 members at present the club has continued to grow. Major alterations were made to the Club House in 1995 to provide better facilities for its female members.

PRICE LIST.

The Hygienic Steam Laundry
(JNO. HARKNESS & COY.),

North Road, BELLSHILL.

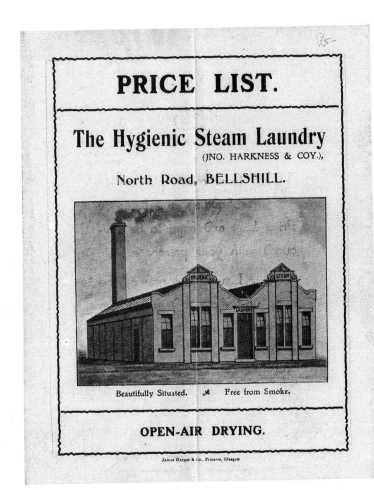

Beautifully Situated.   Free from Smoke.

OPEN-AIR DRYING.

James Harper & Co., Printers, Glasgow

Ladies'.

Aprons	... from 1½d		Stockings	... from	1d
Blouses	„ 4d		„ Silk	„	2d
Chemises	„ 2½d		Handkerchiefs	„	½d
Drawers	„ 2½d		„ Silk or Lace	„	1d
Night Dresses	„ 3d		Underskirts, White	„	6d
Combinations	„ 3d		„ Flannel	„	3d
Slip Bodices	„ 1½d		Night Dress Bags	„	1½d
Towels	„ 1d		Cuffs (per doz.)	„	9d
Dressing Gowns	„ 6d		Collars	„	9d
Morning Dresses	„ 9d		Habit Collars (each)	„	1d

Gentlemen's.

Shirts	... each 3½d		Drawers	... from	2½d
„ with Collar	„ 4d		Semmets	„	2½d
„ Flannel	„ 2½d		Night Shirts	„	2½d
„ Tennis	„ 3d		Pyjama Suits	„	4d
Collars	per doz. 9d		Socks	„	1d
„ Double	„ 9d		Vests	„	6d
Fronts, Plain	from 1d		Ties	„	1d
„ with Collar	„ 1½d		Trousers	... per pair „	1/
Cuffs,	per pair 1d				

Children's.

Sun Bonnets	... from 4d		Wrappers	... from 4d
Sun Hats	„ 6d		Pinafores	„ 2d
Robes	„ 6d			

House Linen.

D'oyleys	... from ½d		Tray Cloths	... from	1d
Curtains	„ 10d		Blankets (per pair)	„	10d
Counterpanes	„ 6d		„ Single	„	5d
Bedroom Towels	per doz. 9d		Sheets	... from	2d
Bath	from 1d		Bolster Slips	„	1½d
Roller	„ 1½d		Pillow	„	1d
Sideboard Cloths	„ 2d		„ Frilled	„	3d
Table Cloths	„ 2d		Blinds (Muslin)	„	2d
Table Napkins	per doz. 9d				

CARPET BEATING, DYEING & FRENCH CLEANING.

CUSTOMER'S GOODS INSURED AGAINST FIRE.

Cleanliness was a serious business in the early 1900s as this price list for the Hygienic Steam Laundry shows. John Harkness established the company in 1905. Originally a director in the local Co-Op, he was renowned as a good businessman and was often asked back to sort out in-house problems. The laundry itself was converted into factory units in 1978 and part of the buildings are still standing on the left-hand side of the North Road.

This circa.1930 picture of Bellshill Salvation Army Band shows Bandmaster Haddow in the middle front row, flanked by Captain and Mrs Ross, the gaffers of the local branch at the time. The band was set up in 1919 as part of General Booth's strategy for making the Salvation Army more active and visible in the community. John Haddow, taking up his post in the early 1920s, was the first commissioned Bandmaster and in sole charge of the band's 28 members. The band is still going strong and the branch celebrates its centenary in 1995.

THE NEW LIBRARY, BELLSHILL.

A. 8428

The first libraries in Bellshill were those at St Andrews' Church Hall and the private circulating library of Reids Newsagent, situated at the west side of Calder Road in Mossend. Bellshill Health Centre and Library was built in the Main Street in 1939 and is presently occupied by Bradshaw Solicitors who bought it from Motherwell District Council in 1992. The new Cultural Centre was built in John Street in 1989, compromising of a library, exhibition areas, meeting rooms, dark room, community hall and cafe.

Now the Alhambra Bar, this public house on the corner of Main Street and Motherwell Road was situated at the original entrance to the Orbiston Estate. At that time, this section of the Motherwell Road would have had sloping gardens and a gatehouse.

12

CROSS GATES, BELLSHILL.

Crossgates was Bellshill's original namesake and this picture from about 1908 holds a wealth of information about its past. The bridge in the middle at the back led through to the Orbiston pits and framed below it are the weavers' shops. Out of the picture at the back left-hand corner was the green at Garden Reach (at the south side on the bend of Hamilton Road) where the first moving pictures in Bellshill were shown in a marquee in 1901. The right-hand side of the picture is taken up mostly with church Glebe lands. The box in the middle beside the trees was a gents' street urinal. On the left-hand side near the middle you can just make out the Strathallan Bar, still servicing Bellshill today. Although a licence was given with no quibbles to the Edinburgh brewers who owned it, the tenement next to it was previously converted into a public bar to no avail. Architect Walter Neilson was refused a licence twice and eventually re-converted the establishment back to its original function.

Unthank Road, pictured here in a 1906 postcard, originally ran up to the farm of the same name. "Unthank" is a common farm name and is thought to be a form of rustic insult aimed at soil which doesn't yield the crops a hard-working farmer thinks he deserves. The farm was taken over by the Mossend Ammunition Works during the First World War and most of the buildings seen here have been demolished.

WEST U.F. CHURCH, BELLSHILL.

Left: Once known as the Toll Church to locals because of its location, this building situated at the north east point of Bellshill Cross has changed its name many times over its history. Since 1929 it has gone by the name of St Andrews. The picture here was taken at the beginning of the century just after it had been amalgamated with the Free churches in 1900 to form the West United Free Church. It was originally known as the Blackmoss Relief Church in 1763 by dissenters who had left the Bothwell Collegiate Church. The early building was demolished and rebuilt in 1846 and, less than a century later, the church was destroyed by fire in 1941. The steeple and walls survived and were re-used in the rebuild. The grave of one William Thompson, a minor poet whose family lived in Bellshill in the late 1800s, can be found in the adjacent cemetery.

Johnstone, Motherwell

Right: By 1887 the number of Lithuanian immigrants in Bellshill was so high that the services of a native priest were required. Reverend Juozas Petrauskis came over in the early 1920s to give spiritual support to his countrymen all over Scotland, producing and editing a weekly paper for Lithuanians in Britain. The community in Bellshill has always attempted to maintain its culture. In 1950 the Lithuanians acquired the Tin Kirk in Mossend for use as a community centre for cultural and social activities such as language classes. The new building in Calder Road is the only Lithuanian Club in Scotland and was donated by the council in 1979. There are presently approximately 1400 people of Lithuanian descent in Bellshill including 300 or so from the first generation.

NEW NORTH ROAD, BELLSHILL

This late 1920s or early 1930s picture shows North Road before it's south end next to the Cross was widened in 1937.

NORTH ROAD, BELLSHILL.

A.8423.

Disinterred remains from the graves which infringed on the site of the modifications were removed to Bothwellpark Cemetery and also to Holytown Church graveyard in 1938. The No 5 Branch Co-op, built in 1920, is now occupied by Dicks Ironmongers and the Bellview Pharmacy.

These disgruntled looking pupils belong to Bellshill Public School which was opened on the 3rd March 1873. Archibald J Noble who died in 1924 would have been the Headmaster at the time this picture was taken in 1913. It is thought by some local historians that the children with the larger white collars could be Lithuanians.

TM Anderson's combined newsagent and hairdressing saloon was located at the east side of Hamilton Road at the Cross. Blacks Ironmonger can just be glimpsed on the left. The Bellshill Speaker, advertised at the front of the shop, was inaugurated in 1892 and started from small beginnings. Its founder, William Combe the printer, originally ran a shop selling newspapers, magazines and books. It was so successful he decided to graduate to publishing himself and set up a printing business at 203-5 Main Street where the Speaker is still published today. Early records were destroyed in a print room fire in 1957. The paper moved out of the Combe family hands in 1950s and has been owned by the Johnstone Press since 1984. A centenary exhibition was held at the Cultural Centre in 1992 and its current circulation is 7-7300.

This picture of Mossend Cross circa 1917 shows the St Margarets Episcopal Mission on the right-hand side. The cross at the front gable can just be made out. The Mission was formed in 1890 and known by locals as the Wee Tin Kirk on account of the unlikely sheets of corrugated iron used to build it. Just behind it, recognisable by its domed roof, is the old theatre which became the Regal cinema. The buildings on the left are still there but a garage now stands roughly where the cinema would have been.

Looking back the other way towards Bellshill, this 1930s view shows the cinema off quite well. Originally known as the Pavilion, its frontage was revamped sometime in the 1930s. The illuminated sign visible here was changed for a more Art Deco one and this canopy above the entrance was removed and replaced by a plainer type.

NEW HOUSING SCHEME, MOSSEND

This view of the new housing development at Mossend (circa 1930) was taken from the bottom of Milnwood pit bing. The chimney stacks of the Beardmore Projectile Works can be seen in the background. Unthank Farm was demolished to make room for Beardmore's shell-making plant during the First World War.

Clydesdale Road, Mossend.

This picture shows a couple of pupils from the nearby Mossend Public School. Sent from Mossend in October 1918, Mary, the writer, tells her friend in St Cyrus that it is very cold and that the lessons are very hard here.

Chimneys from the Milnwood works can be seen in the background. The headmaster at the time would have been William Archibald, known exclusively to all and sundry as Archie Baldie. The old school has since been rebuilt and a roundabout now stands at the junction of Calder Road and Clydesdale Street.

William Austin's bakery was on the North Road opposite the graveyard where the car park is now (see p6 for his building tucked in between Old Mens' Rest and Windsor Place). He won an award for bread making in 1904.

Tom Maxwell's bakery was on the right-hand side of Hamilton Road. A postcard from 1908 or 1909.

The Co-Operative Central Buildings, built in 1911, serviced the Bellshill, Mossend and Holytown areas. It is now occupied by a variety of tenants including an Indian restaurant and a hairdressers. The building has also been re-roofed and the dome at the right removed.

BELLSHILL AND MOSSEND.
CO-OPERATIVE SOCIETY.
ANNUAL GALA. 4/7/1914

A CASE FOR THE AMBULANCE

J. MACDONALD MOTHERWELL

The Bellshill and Mossend Co-Operative Society held annual gala days which were big community events. It is possible that the First Aid team pictured here in 1914 belonged to one of the iron works in the area since the different companies often competed against each other in events like these. At that time there were few GPs available and going to hospital meant a trip to Glasgow.

27

The Academy, Bellshill.

The first school in Bellshill was the Ragged School which was situated in the north side of the West End. Bellshill Academy's primary expansion took place in 1884 and the advanced division was built 15 years later. The site originally held a cottage owned and tenanted by Mr Hogg of Hogg's land in the West End.

Archibald Scott was born in 1852. A joiner by trade, he was involved in building Windsor Place at the Cross before going on to set up a garage and coach building business which became a Limited Company in 1920. He progressed with the times beginning with horse drawn gigs and moving onto trade vehicles including ambulances and lorries such as this one for Steel Coulson the stout brewer. These early lorries were only a small improvement from the horses and carts that they replaced. Their top speed was limited to 12mph and the solid rubber tyres offered little in the way of suspension. The lamps were acetylene powered and a wooden bench sufficed as a seat.

By 1919, when this ambulance was produced, technology had improved considerably and the advances included wire wheels instead of wooden ones, pneumatic tyres (a great comfort for the people this ambulance carried), a proper cab even if the sides were open to the weather, electric lights and more than likely an electric starter motor. In the right background a water cart can be seen. These were used during the summer to damp the roads down and prevent dust blowing everywhere.

In the 1970s and 1980s the company specialised in ice cream vans and exported its wares to far flung climes such as Saudi Arabia and Antigua. When Stewart Scott retired to Carr Bridge he sold the company to a consortium of the workers. The company moved to an industrial estate in East Kilbride but later folded, with the liquidation sale being held in the early 1990s.

Willie Weir set up this pawnbrokers in Mossend in the 1870s. The shop moved down to Main Street, Bellshill when the Mossend area was re-developed in the late 1970s. Weir's still runs by the same name today but sells jewellery now. Pawnbroking has long been given up due to lack of space. Pawnbrokers today need to be able to hold around 8 or 9 six foot safes and the premises at Bellshill were just too small. A branch of Smillie & Weir carries out pawnbroking at a larger shop at Barrhead in Glasgow.

BELLSHILL FIRE BRIGADE. 1912.

Bellshill Fire Station, designed by Alexander Cullen, was built on the site of the original police station in 1911 along with the JP court and new police station. Originally, the fire barrel had to come all the way from Uddingston and was manned by volunteers in the shape of policemen and local tradesmen. The first engine was a Dennis which was later replaced by a Thornycroft model. The new fire station is on the Old Edinburgh Road and is staffed by 29 fire fighters. Bellshill Police Station has taken over the old building on Thorn Road.

C.R. STATION, BELLSHILL.

The Caledonian Railway station was opened in 1879. The wooden station building was originally located at the Hamilton Road end but was moved to the centre of the platform when it was rebuilt later. In 1901 the station master's house was built on the north side of the bridge at Hamilton Road. Tom Maxwell the baker can be seen in the middle of the left platform.

Neilson Street, Bellshill.

Neilson Street circa 1908. The row of tenements beside the Baptist church have gone although the buildings near the top where the street intersects with Hamilton Road are still standing.

West End around 1914. The white building jutting out at the bottom of the street on the left-hand side was the location of Varpas's shop for Lithuanians. The old stagecoach inn, run by John and Janet Craig was in the middle of the street on the right-hand side.

Hamilton Road, Bellshill.

Hamilton Road held a plethora of local businesses. The Caledonian Railway Hotel can be seen on the left hand corner. A funeral parlour, butchers, shoe makers, pub and bakery were among the businesses located on the right hand side of the street. A 1905 view.

HAMILTON ROAD, BELLSHILL

98/57

Looking towards the Cross only about six years later than the preceding picture, there have been many changes. The Cross Mansions have been built and all of the little cottages have been demolished.

DOUGLAS SUPPORT, Bellshill.

Left: Douglas Support 1913. Situated on the north side of the North Calder Water, the Douglas Estate went through several name changes. Originally called "Haggs" (a map of Lanarkshire reveals a shape reminiscent of a witches' profile) the Douglases chose to replace this with the more aesthetic "Rosehall", stolen from one of their other seats in Sutherland. The house was renamed Douglas Support after a 1760s court case over the Douglas succession. The Duke of Hamilton and Archibald Stewart fought a six year case to decide ownership of the estate which Stewart won on appeal. The Duchess of Douglas had supported Archibald financially and the estate and house were renamed in honour of her help.

Right: The sawmill at Douglas Support. The house was demolished earlier this century.

ORBISTON HOUSE.

BRANDON SERIES

Although this postcard is marked as Orbiston House it is nothing of the kind. Boggs Estate was south and west of Orbiston Estate and Boggs Mansion House pictured here was sold to the Douglases in 1819. This building was located where the swing park in Strathclyde Country Park is now. A gable of the fifteenth century Boggs Cotte House is still standing there and was recorded as an Ancient Monument after excavations in 1955.

OLD MILL AT CALDER BRIDGE, BELLSHILL.

The Old Mill, located close to the new bridge at Calder Road, belonged to the Orbiston Estate and dated from ancient times. Mill tolls were used to pay for services at the Orbiston Chapel as early as 1140. The site was later used as a pumping station for Milnwood and Clydesdale works and traces of the mill can still be seen today. It was at one time known as Brig Brae Forge.

Holm Forge, Bellshill

Holm Forge was located on the Motherwell side of the Calder Water. The flax mill would have been at the back on the right of this picture. Abraham Combe stayed in this cottage when the Orbiston Community was set up. A postcard dating from 1908.

Left to right, back row: J Brown, J Mclaren (Captain), P Whellan, J Henderson, R Murray, T McGibbon. Front Row: J Hill, A Anderson, P Friary, D Shanks, J Reid, J Rankin (Assistant Trainer).

At the time this picture was taken in the mid 1930s, Bellshill Athletic was the only Lanarkshire club to have won the Glasgow Junior Cup. Starting off as a juvenile club, it progressed to the junior league and eventually moved to its own grounds at Brandon Park (off Bowling Green Street) in 1903, where it still operates from today. Hughie Gallagher and John Hutton both played for Bellshill Athletic in their younger days.

The District Nurses Cottage on Crossgates Street would have housed around 3 nurses. It is now privately owned.

County Hospital, Bellshill.

Bellshill County Hospital, built in 1870, was initially an infectious disease treatment centre and the fence around it dates from these origins. The hospital was taken over for maternity use in 1899 and later became a childrens hospital in 1917. It is still in operation as a backup to the new multi-storey maternity hospital which was opened off North Road by the Queen in 1962.

This picture of Main Street shows the Brownlie Swan Inn. It is one of the few buildings from this 1911 scene still standing and in use today. Jeannie Brownlie, the original proprietor, died in 1962. Almost opposite was Varpas the Lithuanian shop.

The Cross, Bellshill.

The history of trams in Bellshill stretches over 18 years. The first trams in Mossend and Bellshill ran in 1913 although trams had been running in Motherwell since 1903. By 1929 the decision to abandon tramcars had been taken and the last tram (No.86) arrived at Motherwell Power House from Bellshill Cross on the 14th of February 1931. The day after a new bus service, from Motherwell-Uddingston via New Stevenson and Bellshill, began. Many laments and complaints about the demise of the trams appeared in local papers. The trams had provided cheap travel which was not matched in price by the buses and many families found themselves unable to afford the increased fares. Children who had formerly got the tram to school now found themselves relying on Shank's pony.

A 1940s view of Bellshill Main Street. With petrol rationing still in effect, the roads were remarkably quiet then.

Belvidere School, Bellshill.

These children look happily free from the pressing concerns of homework. Belvidere School is between Motherwell Road and Crossgates road and is still standing today.

The New Calder Bridge was built in 1927 and replaced the old stone arch bridge. The old bridge had been rebuilt at some point before 1915 and in the process had been widened.

Alex Hamilton laid the foundation stone at the Baptist Church on the 2nd of December in 1910. The new Cultural Centre is situated directly across from it. Behind the church was the Caledonian Railway station.

THE CROSS, BELLSHILL

Bellshill Cross decorated for the Coronation of 1937.